Brer Fox captured Brer Terrapin and carried him off in a bag. But Brer Rabbit was watching and guessed that Brer Fox was playing a trick on someone. So he thought of a plan to rescue Brer Terrapin and teach Brer Fox a lesson.

A collection of the popular Brer Rabbit stories written by Enid Blyton

ENID BLYTON

BRER RABBIT saves Brer Terrapin

Illustrated by Val Biro

KNIGHT BOOKS
Hodder & Stoughton

ISBN 0 340 19117 1

First published in 1948 by
Latimer House Limited
This edition first published 1976
by Knight, the paperback division of
Hodder & Stoughton Children's Books,
Salisbury Road, Leicester

Printed and bound in Great Britain by
Cox & Wyman Ltd, London, Reading and Fakenham

Contents

Brer Rabbit saves Brer Terrapin

ONE time Brer Fox was going down the big road and he saw old Brer Terrapin going to his home. Now Brer Fox knew Brer Terrapin was a good friend to Brer Rabbit, and it seemed to him it was a mighty good time to catch him. Brer Fox didn't have any kindly feelings towards people who were friends of Brer Rabbit.

Brer Fox ran back to his own house, which was not far off, and got a bag. Then he ran down the road again, rushed up behind Brer Terrapin, caught him up and threw him into the bag. He slung the bag across his back, then off he went, galloping home.

Brer Terrapin, he shouted, but it wasn't any good. He wriggled and struggled, but that wasn't any good either. Brer Fox just went on going, and there was old Brer Terrapin in the corner of the bag, and the bag tied up hard and fast.

But where was Brer Rabbit whilst all this was going on? Where was that long-eared, hoppetty-skippetty creature, that up-and-down-and-sailing-round Brer Rabbit? He wasn't far off, you may be sure!

Brer Fox went trotting down the big road with the bag on his back – and Brer Rabbit was sitting in the bushes just by the side of the road. He saw Brer Fox trotting by and he saw the bag on his back too.

'Now what's Brer Fox got in that bag?' said Brer Rabbit to himself. 'I don't know what it can be.'

Well, Brer Rabbit sat in the bushes and wondered and wondered, but the more he wondered the less he could think what it was. He watched Brer Fox a-trotting down the road, and still he sat in the bushes and wondered.

'Huh!' said Brer Rabbit at last. 'Brer Fox has no business to be trotting down the road carrying something other people don't know about. I guess I'll go after Brer Fox and find out what's in the bag!'

With that, Brer Rabbit set out. He hadn't got a bag to carry and he went mighty quickly. He took a short cut, and by the time Brer Fox got to his house Brer Rabbit had had time to get into his strawberry-bed and trample down a whole lot of plants. When he had done that, he sat down in some bushes where he could see Brer Fox coming home.

By and by Brer Fox came along with his bag across his back. He unlatched his door, he did, and then he threw Brer Terrapin down in a corner in the bag, and sat down to rest himself, for Brer Terrapin was mighty heavy to carry.

Brer Fox had hardly put a match to his pipe when Brer Rabbit stuck his head in at the door and shouted, 'Brer Fox! Oh, Brer Fox! You'd better take your stick and run out yonder. Coming along just now I heard a fuss going on in your garden, and I looked round and there were a whole lot of folk in your strawberry-bed, just a-trampling the strawberries down! I shouted at them, but they didn't take any notice of a little man like me. Make haste, Brer Fox, make haste! Get your stick and run. I'd go with you too, but I've got to get home. You'd better hurry, Brer Fox, if you want to save your strawberries. Run, Brer Fox, run!'

With that Brer Rabbit darted back into the bushes, and Brer Fox dropped his pipe and grabbed his stick and rushed out to his strawberry-bed. And no sooner was he gone than old Brer Rabbit hopped out of the bushes and into the house.

He didn't make a bit of noise. He looked round and there was the bag in the corner. He caught hold of it and felt it to see what was inside. And suddenly something yelled, 'Ow! Go away! Let me alone! Turn me loose! Ow!'

Brer Rabbit jumped back astonished. Then before you could wink an eye he slapped himself on the leg and laughed out loud.

'If I'm not making a mistake, that's nobody's voice but old Brer Terrapin's!' said Brer Rabbit.

'Is that Brer Rabbit?' yelled Brer Terrapin.

'It is,' said Brer Rabbit.

'Then hurry up and get me out,' said Brer Terrapin. 'There's dust in my throat, grit in my eyes, and I can hardly breathe. Get me out, Brer Rabbit.'

'Heyo, Brer Terrapin,' said Brer Rabbit. 'You're a lot smarter than I am – because here you are in a bag and I don't know how in the name of goodness you've tied yourself up in there, that I don't!'

Brer Terrapin tried to explain and Brer Rabbit kept on laughing, but all the same he untied the bag, took Brer Terrapin out and carried him outside the gate. Then, when he had done this, Brer Rabbit ran off to where he knew some wasps had a nest just about as big as a football.

The wasp-nest was in a hollow tree. Brer Rabbit slipped in at the bottom of the tree and there was the nest inside. He slapped his paw over the hole where the wasps went in and out, knocked the nest down into his bag, and there he had it, wasps and all!

Then back he raced to Brer Fox's house and flung the bag down on the floor, tied up fast. Well, the way he slammed that bag down on the floor stirred all those wasps up and put them into a very bad temper! They buzzed fit to make holes in the bag!

Soon Brer Rabbit saw Brer Fox coming down the back-garden, where he had been looking for the folks that had trodden down his strawberries. He had been putting the plants straight and picking off the squashed fruit, and Brer Fox was feeling mighty mad about it too.

By the time Brer Fox got indoors Brer Rabbit was off and away into a bush – and there he sat with old Brer Terrapin, waiting to see what would happen.

Brer Fox went indoors, hitting the ground with his stick, and vowing that he would shake Brer Terrapin to bits, he was in such a bad temper.

He slammed the door and Brer Rabbit and Brer Terrapin waited. They listened, but at first they couldn't hear anything. By and by they heard the most tremendous noise!

'Seems like a whole crowd of cows running round and round inside Brer Fox's house,' Brer Rabbit said to Brer Terrapin.

'I can hear chairs a-falling,' said Brer Terrapin.

'I can hear the table turning over,' said Brer Rabbit.

'I can hear the crockery smashing,' said Brer Terrapin.

'Huh!' said Brer Rabbit, enjoying himself. 'Brer Fox must be having a fine game with those wasps. What a surprise he got when he opened the bag to get you – and found a wasp's nest instead!'

Just as Brer Rabbit said that, Brer Fox's door flew wide open and out rushed Brer Fox, squalling and howling as if two hundred dogs had got him by the tail!

He ran straight to the river, he did, and plunged in to get rid of the wasps on him.

Brer Rabbit and Brer Terrapin sat there in the bushes and laughed and laughed, till by and

by Brer Rabbit rolled over and said, 'One more laugh, Brer Terrapin, and you'll have to carry me home!'

'Get on my back then, Brer Rabbit, get on my back,' said Brer Terrapin. 'I'll carry you all right. Shoo! That will teach Brer Fox not to go a-catching an old fellow like me and putting him into a dusty bag!'

Brer Fox came out of the river at last – but to this day he doesn't know how it was that though he put old Brer Terrapin into a bag, it was a nest of wasps that came out! And you may be sure Brer Rabbit never told him!

Brer Wolf tries to grow horns

It came about one day that all the creatures that had horns made up their minds to meet together and have a talk about how to take care of themselves – because the creatures that had teeth and claws were snatching the horned animals round every corner!

So the horned animals sent out word all round the countryside, and planned a meeting in the woods. When the day came, what a large crowd of them there was! They stamped through the bushes, they bellowed and they mooed, they grunted and they snorted. My, it was a fine crowd that met together that day.

Mr Bull, he was there, and he took the head of the meeting. Mr Steer was there, stamping his hoof. Mrs Cow was there, whisking her tail round. Mr Billy Goat was there, wagging his beard and talking away to Mrs Cow. Mr

Unicorn was there, with his great long horn sticking right up into the air. Mr Benjamin Ram was there, with his fiddle. And old man Rhinoceros was there too, taking up a mighty lot of room.

There were lots more, too many to tell, for they came in crowds. Old Brer Wolf, he heard about this meeting and he made up his mind he'd go along and see what it was all about – and maybe sneak off with one of Mr Benjamin Ram's children.

But he didn't know how to go without being known as Brer Wolf. Any creature there without horns would be noticed at once and sent away with a horn in his side if he wasn't careful! So Brer Wolf sat down and thought hard. He meant to go to that meeting – but how could he go there unnoticed?

Pretty soon he grinned to himself and went out to the woods. He cut himself two crooked sticks and tied them on his head! The sticks looked just like horns, and Brer Wolf looked a mighty queer creature! He set off to the meeting, and mixed with all the crowd.

Now as he went to the meeting Brer Rabbit

saw him – and he sprang aside into the bushes quickly when he saw a creature looking like Brer Wolf, yet carrying horns on his head! 'My!' said Brer Rabbit to himself, 'if it isn't enough that Brer Wolf's got claws and teeth – and now he's got horns as well. I wonder why.'

Well, Brer Rabbit didn't mean to let Brer Wolf out of his sight, so he went after him, hiding in the bushes all the way. And pretty soon he came to the meeting too, but as he had no horns on his head Brer Rabbit kept in the bushes, and lay there without moving even an ear.

When Brer Wolf got to the meeting Mr Bull saw him.

'Who are you?' said Mr Bull, in surprise, for he had never seen a creature quite like Brer Wolf before.

'Baa-aa-aa!' said Brer Wolf. 'I'm little Sooky Calf.'

Well, Mr Bull looked at Brer Wolf very hard over the tops of his spectacles, and Brer Wolf he put down his head and made little bleating noises as best he could. But just then someone called Mr Bull away, and Brer Wolf took his place among the crowd, sniffing and smelling everyone.

By and by the creatures began talking and telling each other of the bad ways of toothed and clawed animals. Whilst all this was going on, a big horse-fly came sailing around, and Brer Wolf quite forgot that he was supposed to be a horned creature, and he did what no horned animal ever does – he snapped at that fly!

All this time Brer Rabbit had been hiding in the bushes watching Brer Wolf, and when he saw Brer Wolf snap at the horse-fly he laughed out loud.

Mr Bull heard the laugh and he bellowed out angrily, 'Who's that laughing away, and showing bad manners at this meeting?'

Nobody answered at all, and there was a silence. Then Brer Rabbit shouted out:

'Oh, kittle-kattle, kittle-kattle, where are your eyes?
Whoever saw a Sooky Calf snapping at flies?'

The horned animals all looked at one another and wondered what this meant. Brer Wolf felt mighty angry with Brer Rabbit, but he couldn't do a thing about it.

Before very long something bit Brer Wolf on the back of his neck, and before he knew what he was doing he sat right down and scratched himself well with his hind foot – a thing that no cow or bull ever did!

Well, Brer Rabbit shouted with laughter once more to see him, and disturbed the meeting again. Mr Bull bellowed away in anger – and as soon as he had stopped and there was a dead silence, Brer Rabbit sang out at the top of his voice again:

'Scritchum-scratchum, look at his paws,
See that Sooky Calf scratching with claws!'

Brer Wolf was mighty scared, but it didn't seem as if any of the horned creatures knew what Brer Rabbit meant, for they took no notice of him at all.

Brer Wolf sat down on the ground behind Mr Benjamin Ram, hoping that Mr Ram would hide him well from Mr Bull's eye. He put his long tail out behind him, and Sis Cow stepped on it by mistake. Brer Wolf gave a yell, and Brer Rabbit gave a great shout of laughter again.

'Who's that a-laughing and a-spoiling the

meeting?' roared Mr Bull. Nobody spoke a word – and then old Brer Rabbit he shouted loudly again from where he was hidden in the bushes:

'Rinkum, sinkum, ride him on a rail,
That Sooky Calf's got a long, bushy tail!'

Brer Wolf crouched down behind Mr Benjamin Ram and tried to hide his tail. Nobody seemed to take much notice of him – except Mr Bull – and he had his eye on Brer Wolf all right! Yes – Brer Wolf noticed that Mr Bull was looking straight at him, and he didn't like it a bit. He felt mighty scared!

The meeting went on, but Brer Wolf felt more and more scared because he saw Mr Bull edging nearer and nearer to him through the crowd. And Brer Rabbit, he wasn't going to be quiet, not he! He shouted out at the top of his voice:

'One and one never can make six,
Sticks aren't horns, and horns aren't sticks!'

And just about then Mr Bull saw that Brer Wolf's horns weren't horns at all but two bits of crooked stick! He roared in a rage and ran straight at Brer Wolf. He put down his head, he did, and he ran at Brer Wolf like a thunderbolt.

Brer Wolf gave a yelp and tore away. Mr Bull grazed his horns against Brer Wolf's sides and gave him two good cuts. My, how Brer Wolf jumped!

He rushed away from the meeting, and he was so mad with Brer Rabbit that he reckoned he would pretend that the wounds Mr Bull had given him had killed him. So he sent word round that he was dead.

Well, Brer Rabbit thought it might well be so, for he had seen Mr Bull's horns going straight at Brer Wolf. And he thought he would pop round to Brer Wolf's house and see if he really was dead. But he remembered how Brer Wolf had tried to trick him that way before, and he didn't go inside the house – he only put his head round the door and peeped in.

Brer Rabbit saw some of the other creatures there, and he said 'howdy' to them. Then he said, 'Poor Brer Wolf! So Mr Bull killed him! Dear, dear! Tell me, folks, has Brer Wolf grinned yet?'

'No, Brer Wolf hasn't grinned,' said the creatures there. 'Why ever should he grin, Brer Rabbit?'

'Ah,' said Brer Rabbit, 'wolves are strange creatures, folks. They aren't dead till they grin. You tell me when Brer Wolf grins and I'll know he's dead for good.'

Well, when Brer Wolf heard this, he wanted Brer Rabbit to think he was dead, so he grinned from ear to ear! And then, of course, Brer Rabbit knew he was alive all right, and he picked up his hat and stick and ran off for home – and every now and again he would sit down and laugh fit to kill himself!

Brer Terrapin gets some fish

BRER TERRAPIN didn't mind if he lived on land or in the water, and it was mighty useful to him sometimes to be able to slide into the river when he wanted to get out of somebody's way. But it wasn't any use sliding into the water when Brer Mink was about, because Brer Mink could jump into the river and swim and dive till he began to think nobody could beat him at it!

Now one day Brer Mink was going along by the riverside with a nice string of fish swinging on his stick, when who should he come across but Old Brer Terrapin? Everyone teased Brer Terrapin, he was such a queer old one-and-six-pence, and most folks thought he was as woolly-headed as a silly old sheep. But Brer Terrapin was smarter than a good many!

'Heyo, Brer Mink!' said Brer Terrapin. 'Where did you get that nice string of fish?'

Brer Mink was feeling very proud of himself those days, and he grinned down at Brer

Terrapin. 'Heyo, old stick-in-the-mud,' he said. 'Where do you suppose I got the fish – up in the meadow? I got them down in the river, of course.'

Brer Terrapin looked astonished.

'Well, well, well, Brer Mink!' he said. 'Down in the river, you say? Who'd have believed it?'

'Oh, I'm mighty good in the water, Brer

Terrapin,' said Brer Mink, talking very biggitty.

'That's so, Brer Mink,' said Brer Terrapin. 'But bless gracious, if a landsman like you starts going into the water what's going to happen to the water-folks? It looks all wrong to me, Brer Mink, you taking to the water like this!'

'Looks or no looks, I'm going to catch fish if I want to,' said Brer Mink.

Brer Terrapin swayed his head from side to side and said, 'Brer Mink, you don't mean to say you can swim under the water and catch fish that way? You don't mean to say you can keep under long enough to do that?'

'Oh, that's easy enough,' said Brer Mink, still talking mighty biggitty. '*You* might find it difficult, old stick-in-the-mud.'

'Don't call me old stick-in-the-mud,' said Brer Terrapin, offended.

'All right, old stick-in-the-mud,' said Brer Mink, and he gave Brer Terrapin's shell a poke with his stick. Brer Terrapin began to feel mighty mad, and he swayed his head from side to side again. But he still spoke very sweetly and kindly to Brer Mink.

'Well, Brer Mink,' said Brer Terrapin, 'I'd

like to see you swim under the water, that I would. I'm a landsman myself, I am, and it's a long time since I got my feet wet, but I don't mind going into the water with you and having a match to see who can keep under the longest. No, I don't mind that at all. I expect you'll beat me, but never mind that.'

'Huh!' said Brer Mink, pleased. 'Beat you? Of course I'll beat you, old stick-in-the-mud! Yes – and that's all you'll do too – just stick right down in the mud – and I'll have to get you out! Come along and we'll see what you do.'

'We'll go down into the river,' said Brer Terrapin, 'and the one that can stay under the water the longest can walk off with that string of fish of yours!'

'Huh!' said Brer Mink, 'you don't really think you'd get that, do you, Brer Terrapin? Come on now and I'll show you what a fine fellow Brer Mink is!'

The two of them went to the edge of the water. Brer Mink laid down his string of fish on the bank. Then he and Brer Terrapin began to wade into the water.

'Ow, Brer Mink!' said Brer Terrapin, pretending not to like the water at all. 'Ow! This water feels mighty cold, and it isn't any higher than my waist yet. Goodness knows how I'll feel when it's up to my chin!'

'Come on, Brer Terrapin, come on,' said Brer Mink. 'If you don't hurry we'll never get to the deep part!'

Well, they waded right in, and Brer Terrapin, who was pretending to shiver with the cold, said, 'Now then, Brer Mink, we'll dive down, and the one that stays under the longest is the one that gets the fish!'

'That's right,' said Brer Mink.

'Go!' said Brer Terrapin, and under they both went. Of course Brer Terrapin could stay under the water far longer than Brer Mink, and Brer Mink ought to have known it. They stayed under and they stayed under till by and by Brer Mink simply *had* to come up for breath, and mighty glad he was to be at the top of the water again, for he was pretty nearly bursting for want of air.

Then, after a while, Brer Terrapin stuck his nose out of the water.

'Heyo, Brer Terrapin – seems you've beaten

me!' said Brer Mink, in the greatest astonishment.

'Well, well!' said Brer Terrapin, as if he felt surprised too. 'We'll make it the best out of three, Brer Mink. We'll have three dives, and the one that wins twice shall have the fish! If I beat you this time, then the fish are mine. If I get beaten, then we'll have a third trial.'

With that, down they went – but Brer Mink, he made up his mind that even if Brer Terrapin won he wouldn't have the fish! No – he'd pick them up from the bank and gallop off through the woods with them, and that old stick-in-the-mud of a Brer Terrapin wouldn't be able to catch him. Brer Mink grinned to himself as he went under for the second time.

Brer Terrapin saw the grin – and he knew what Brer Mink was thinking. So Brer Terrapin he just dived a little way under the water and then came up at once again. And whilst old Brer Mink was still under the water, gasping for air, Brer Terrapin gobbled up every single one of the fish!

Brer Mink came up at last, and as he came up Brer Terrapin slid down under the water again,

and he slid so smoothly that he didn't leave even a bubble! He didn't stay there very long though – he came up quickly, and panted and puffed at the top as if he'd been down for hours and hadn't any breath left at all!

Well, old Brer Terrapin came up, he did, and Brer Mink yelled out that he'd beaten him again. But before Brer Mink could say another word Brer Terrapin took a look round at the bank and yelled out, 'You're a rascal, Brer Mink, that's what you are, you're a rascal!'

'What have I done now, Brer Terrapin?' asked Brer Mink in astonishment.

'Don't ask *me*, Brer Mink! Look up there on the bank where you've been eating those fish, and then ask yourself what you've done! You're a rascal, you are!'

Brer Mink looked round and, sure enough, the fish were gone. Old Brer Terrapin kept on talking.

'You came up first, didn't you, Brer Mink, and while I was down there in the water, bursting for air, you were sitting up here chewing up the fish which should have been mine, because I've won them!'

'I *didn't* eat the fish!' said Brer Mink. 'I tell you I didn't, Brer Terrapin.'

'Well, who did then?' said Brer Terrapin. 'Who did then? Tell me that, Brer Mink. I can't see any one around for miles that could have taken those fish and eaten them.'

Brer Mink, he climbed up the bank and looked all around too – but he couldn't see any one either.

'Well, I just don't believe you, Brer Mink,' said Brer Terrapin. 'You've tricked me, you have. You said I was an old stick-in-the-mud, as woolly-headed as a silly sheep – and it seems as if you're right, Brer Mink, so it does. You've tricked me properly. If you go on like this you'll be worse than Brer Rabbit!'

Now when Brer Terrapin told Brer Mink he was nearly as bad as Brer Rabbit, Brer Mink felt proud, because every one knew that Brer Rabbit was the cunningest and smartest creature of the lot. So Brer Mink gave a laugh, he did, as if he knew a lot more than he was going to tell, and he poked Brer Terrapin on the shell.

'All right, all right, Brer Mink,' said Brer Terrapin, shuffling off. 'I'm not going to get mad with you, because I think it's a mighty clever trick you played, but all the same you ought to be ashamed of yourself for tricking an old stick-in-the-mud like me, so you ought!'

And with that Brer Terrapin went off, but after he got out of sight he drew back into his house and laughed and laughed till he nearly cracked his shell! He wasn't such an old stick-in-the-mud as Brer Mink thought!

Brer Fox's fish-trap

ONE year there was a very dry summer, and the rivers and ponds got dried up so that there was hardly any drinking-water to be found. Even the big river got low, and as for the streams, some of them disappeared altogether.

The animals all had to go to the big river to drink. They met there, and the biggest ones drank first, and they drank so much that there was hardly any left for the little ones.

Brer Rabbit didn't mind very much. He always knew how to look after himself, and if anyone was going to get water it was old Brer Rabbit. The other creatures saw his footprints by the riverside and they waited for him, but they never caught him.

Brer Fox wasn't so lucky. He always seemed to go for a drink when Mr Lion and Brer Bull and the big creatures were there, and they crowded him out and chased him away. So poor Brer Fox, he was always thirsty and he didn't know what to do about it.

'I'll go along to Brer Rabbit's house and see how he manages to get a drink,' said Brer Fox to himself, and off he set.

Brer Rabbit was at home. He was sitting outside his front door singing a little song:

'Oh, Mister Rabbit, your eye's mighty big!
Yes, sir, yes! It's made for me to see!
Oh, Mr Rabbit, your tail's mighty short,
Yes, sir, yes! But it just fits me!'

'Howdy, Brer Rabbit?' said Brer Fox.

'Howdy, Brer Fox?' said Brer Rabbit. 'What are you wanting this morning? You look mighty down in the mouth.'

'Brer Rabbit, I can't seem to get anything to drink,' said Brer Fox. 'When I go to the big river Mr Lion roars at me, and Brer Bull crowds me out, and the rest of them chase me away. Now, you're a smart fellow, Brer Rabbit – can't you tell me how to get a drink when I want one?

Well, Brer Rabbit, he sat and thought hard for a few minutes, then he grinned. 'Oh yes, Brer Fox,' he said, 'I can tell you what to do.

You've come to the right man for help, you have.'

'What shall I do then, Brer Rabbit?' asked Brer Fox.

'You go home and rub some treacle over yourself,' said Brer Rabbit. 'Then go out into the woods and roll over and over in some leaves. They will stick to the treacle, and you'll be covered from head to foot with them.'

'What shall I do after that?' asked Brer Fox, in astonishment.

'Well, you go down to the river and hide in a bush,' said Brer Rabbit. 'And when the creatures all come to get a drink, you jump out at them, Brer Fox – and you'll scare them all into the middle of next week!'

'Huh!' said Brer Fox. 'That sounds mighty good to me, Brer Rabbit. I always said you were a smart fellow!'

'I haven't finished yet,' said Brer Rabbit, who was really enjoying himself. 'After you've scared everyone away, go and wallow in the water and drink all you like – and pretty soon, Brer Fox, the fishes will all come swimming up to get a bite of treacle, and you'll be able to catch as many as you want to. And, if you're a nice fellow, Brer Fox, I'll take it kindly of you if you'll bring me one of the fish for myself.'

'I'll do that, Brer Rabbit,' promised Brer Fox. 'Yes, I'll surely do that.'

With that off he ran home. He went to his cupboard and took down a jar of treacle. He smeared it all over himself from head to foot – and a mighty sticky mess he looked when he had finished! Then he went out into the woods and rolled over and over in the leaves and rubbish there till he looked as odd as could be!

When Brer Fox was ready he went down to the river and hid himself. By and by all the creatures came along to drink the water, and whilst they were a-pushing and a-scuffling and a-snuffling, Brer Fox, he jumped out of the bushes at them, and switched himself round and round, squealing loudly.

Well, all the creatures looked at this odd thing and they didn't know what to make of it at all! Brer Wolf saw him first and he was so startled that he jumped right over Brer Bear's head to get away! Brer Bear shot backwards, yelling, 'Who's that? Who's that?'

Then everyone saw the odd-looking creature and rushed away like apples rolling downhill, and before Brer Fox had time to do a few more squeals he had the river to himself!

The creatures didn't go very far. They soon stopped and looked round. Then they began to creep back a little nearer, trying to make out what this fearsome-looking thing was that had given them such a fright. When they got near enough to see, there was Brer Fox walking up and down, up and down, switching his tail about and squealing whenever he thought about it.

The animals didn't know what to think at all. They watched, and Brer Fox marched up and down. Still they watched and still he marched up and down. It went on like this till Brer Fox thought it was about time he made himself into a fish-trap and wallowed in the water as Brer Rabbit had said. Then the fishes would come up to him for a bite of treacle and he'd get an armful of them.

So Brer Fox marched into the water and lay down in it. He rolled over and over and wallowed in it, watching for the fishes to come.

But they didn't come and they didn't come.

Brer Fox didn't know what Brer Rabbit knew! Brer Rabbit knew that as soon as Brer Fox went into the water the river would wash away the leaves and the dirt and the treacle – and there would be Brer Fox, plain for anyone to see!

Well, the water washed away the treacle, and off went the leaves and the dirt downstream, and there was Brer Fox, just himself and nobody odd at all!

The animals were all watching Brer Fox rolling in the water – and bless gracious, how they stared when they saw the leaves floating off him and saw that he was just Brer Fox! Then they knew he had played a trick on them and they were mighty wild.

'Brer Wolf! Brer Wolf!' yelled Brer Bear. 'You head him off down there, and I'll head him off up here. We'll catch Brer Fox sure as a fly's got wings!'

Brer Fox, rolling in the water, still watching for the fish that didn't come, heard Brer Bear's voice, and looked up to see what the fuss was about. When he saw Brer Bear coming one way and Brer Wolf coming another, he jumped out of the river in a mighty hurry. He took a look down at himself and saw that the treacle and leaves had gone – and then off he went as if a hive of bees were on his tail.

He wasn't any too soon. As it was, Brer Bear

got the tip-end of his tail – another moment and he'd have caught him!

Brer Fox went home through the woods, wet and angry. As he passed Brer Rabbit's house he saw him out in the porch, rocking himself in a rocking-chair and singing his song:

'*Oh, Mister Rabbit, your ears are mighty long!*
Yes, sir, yes! My ears are made to last!
Oh, Mister Rabbit, your teeth are mighty sharp!
Yes, sir, yes! They cut down the grass!'

Brer Fox was going by without a word, but Brer Rabbit saw him. 'Heyo, Brer Fox!' he shouted. 'Have you brought me a fish from your fish-trap?'

But Brer Fox, he didn't answer a word. He gave Brer Rabbit one look, and if looks could have killed – well, Brer Rabbit would have dropped down dead, there isn't a doubt of that!

Brer Fox tries another fish-trap

Now although Brer Fox was very angry with Brer Rabbit for tricking him into making himself a fish-trap, he couldn't help thinking it certainly would be a mighty fine idea to make a real fish-trap. So he set to work to make one.

Brer Rabbit saw him working away at the trap and he walked over to see him.

'What are you making, Brer Fox?' he said.

'A fish-trap,' said Brer Fox, rather proud of himself. 'Why don't you make one too, Brer Rabbit? Fish is a change from fresh meat and salad.'

'Thank you very much, Brer Fox,' said Brer Rabbit politely, 'but I'm not wanting fish for dinner just now, and anyway I'm too busy to make fish-traps.'

Well, Brer Fox, he finished his fish-trap at last, and then he went in his boat up and down the river hunting for a good place to put it.

He hunted and he hunted and at last he found the right place. He put his trap there and set it.

Then he rubbed his hands in delight and thought of all the fish he would catch. He didn't know that Brer Rabbit was sitting on the bank under a bush, watching him fix that trap. No – if Brer Fox had known that, he wouldn't have felt quite so happy.

Brer Rabbit watched Brer Fox carry stones and rocks to put on his trap to hold it in place. He grinned to see Brer Fox getting hotter and hotter.

Brer Fox felt very tired after all his hard work. He went home, washed his face and hands, and sat down to rest. After he had taken a good long rest he went down to the river to see if he had caught any fish in his trap. He was rather afraid of water-snakes when he put his hand in the trap but all the same he felt all round the trap to see if he could feel any fish – and there were none there at all.

So back home he went once more. 'I guess I must wait a few days before I go and look again,' said Brer Fox. 'I'll go down to my trap at the end of the week.' So towards the week-end he went down to his trap, felt all round it, and was mighty disappointed to find no fish there.

It went on like this till Brer Fox was quite tired of running to and from his fish-trap and never finding a thing there. And one day, when he was looking around his trap, he saw foot-prints that told him someone had been along there.

'Yes, someone's been robbing my fish-trap,' said Brer Fox. 'And if I don't make any mistake I sort of know who that someone is!'

He got into his boat, paddled it to an overhanging bush nearby and slid under it with his boat so that he was quite hidden. He watched all the morning. Nobody came. He watched all dinner-time and after, and nobody came. Towards the evening, just as Brer Fox was making ready to come out from under the bush and slip off home, he heard a noise by the fish-trap. He peeped out – and there was old Brer Rabbit in a boat, poling it along to the trap.

Brer Rabbit wasn't using a paddle to get his boat along, as Brer Fox did – no, he was standing up in his boat and using a long pole to push it along, just as we do when we are punting. Old Brer Rabbit, he stood in the back part of the boat, pushed his pole to the bottom of the river, gave it a shove, and sent his boat along at a good speed.

Brer Fox felt mighty mad when he saw this, and he watched and waited. 'I'll just wait till Brer Rabbit comes by me and then I'll go after him in my boat and catch him!' said Brer Fox.

'I guess I can paddle my boat quicker than he can pole his!'

Brer Rabbit poled right up to the fish-trap, bent down and put his paw into it. He pulled out a great big fish – then he reached in and pulled out another fish, then he pulled out a

third, and it went on like this till he had got his boat almost full of fish from Brer Fox's fish-trap!

Just about then Brer Fox paddled his boat out from under his bush and came towards Brer Rabbit.

'Ay-yi, Brer Rabbit!' yelled Brer Fox. 'You're the man that's been robbing my fish-trap all this time! I've got you this time! Oh, you needn't try to run! I've got you this time for sure!'

Brer Rabbit jumped round and saw Brer Fox. He flung the last fish into his boat, grabbed for his pole and started off, with Brer Fox just behind him. Now Brer Fox could paddle much faster than Brer Rabbit could pole, and Brer Rabbit knew this – but did he care? Not a bit of it! Old Brer Rabbit had a trick up his sleeve all right. He had more fun in getting away from Brer Fox that time than ever he had before in all his life!

How old Brer Bull-Frog laughed to see what happened! He was a-sitting there on the bank and he saw it all. Brer Rabbit had to stand at the back of his boat to pole it – and as soon as Brer Fox's boat touched his, Brer Rabbit took his pole and pushed hard at Brer Fox's boat. And the harder he pushed, the farther forward he sent himself and the farther backward went Brer Fox! Oh, it looked mighty easy to old Brer Bull-Frog sitting on the bank there, and all Brer Fox could do was to shake his fist and grit his teeth – but he couldn't get in front of Brer Rabbit's boat, no matter how he tried.

And when Brer Fox stopped to smack Brer Bull-Frog on the nose for laughing so much, Brer Rabbit slipped ahead, landed on the bank, took up the fish, and raced for home. Oh no, Brer Fox, you can't catch old Brer Rabbit!

Brer Rabbit's pond

At the back of Brer Rabbit's house was a round pond. Sometimes, when it got very dirty with leaves falling into it, Brer Rabbit cleaned it out.

One time he cleaned it out beautifully, and then he stood and sighed by the edge of his empty pond.

'If only the rain would come and fill it!' he groaned to himself. 'If the rain doesn't come I'll have to fill my big watering-can fifty times and carry it from the tap to the pond!'

Well, the rain didn't come. The sun shone out, and the sky was as blue as forget-me-nots. Not a rain-cloud was to be seen!

'It's no good!' said Brer Rabbit at last. 'I'll have to fill the pond myself.' So he picked up his big watering-can and filled it at the tap by the side of his house.

He dragged it to the pond and emptied the water in – slishy-sloshy, slishy-sloshy! It made a lovely noise. Brer Terrapin came by, and looked over the wall when he heard the noise.

'My!' he said to Brer Rabbit. 'That's a fine game you're having this morning! It's fun to play with water like that. Let me have a turn.'

'You can't drag my big watering-can along, old slow-coach!' said Brer Rabbit. But Brer Terrapin soon showed him that he could! He balanced the big can on his back and walked slowly to the pond. He stood with his back to the pond and jerked the can. It poured all the water out at once.

'My, but it's heavy!' panted Brer Terrapin. 'I guess you've got a hard job this morning, Brer Rabbit. Why don't you get your friends to come along and help you?'

'Huh! As if Brer Fox and Brer Wolf would fill my pond for me!' said Brer Rabbit.

'You let me manage things for you,' said Brer Terrapin with a sly grin. 'You let me manage things, Brer Rabbit. You've always been a good friend to me, and if you'll let me have a swim in your pond now and again, I'll just see if I can't get you a bit of help this morning!'

'All right, Brer Terrapin, you try,' said Brer Rabbit, and he watched Brer Terrapin crawling out of his gate.

Well, Brer Terrapin, he went down the road, and soon he met Brer Fox.

'Heyo, old shellyback, where have you been this long time?' said Brer Fox.

'Oh, I've just come from Brer Rabbit's,' said Brer Terrapin. 'And he gave me such a treat! He let me help him pour water into his pond! It went slishy-sloshy, slishy-sloshy into the empty pond, a real treat to see it! It's fun to play with water, isn't it, Brer Fox? But it's no use *you* going along to Brer Rabbit's, for I don't suppose he'll give you a treat like that. It's only because I'm a friend of his.'

'Well, I'm a friend of his too!' said Brer Fox. 'Haven't I known him for years and years? I guess we've done more things together than any other creatures in the world. If I want to pour water into his pond, I just *know* he'd let me!'

'All right, you go and see, Brer Fox,' said Brer Terrapin, putting his head inside his shell to grin to himself. 'You go and see!'

So Brer Fox went along to Brer Rabbit's, and

he soon heard Brer Rabbit singing, 'Hi ho! Hi ho!' and he heard the sound of water splashing merrily into the pond.

'Heyo, Brer Rabbit!' yelled Brer Fox. 'You seem to be mighty busy this morning. That's a fine job you're doing.'

'Oh, a mighty fine job!' said Brer Rabbit, winking to himself. 'A job that everyone would like to do, Brer Fox. I just gave Brer Terrapin a turn at it, because he's a very old friend of mine, and I like giving him a treat.'

'Well, I'm an old friend of yours too,' said Brer Fox. 'You let me have a turn as well, Brer Rabbit. I don't like Brer Terrapin going around saying he's the only friend of yours that helps you with your pond. You let me have a turn too.'

'Why, Brer Fox, I'd be pleased to,' said Brer Rabbit. 'Yes, yes, you have a turn – have two turns – have ten turns if you want to! I'm not one to be selfish. No – if my friends want a share in my pleasures, they are welcome to them. You take the can, Brer Fox, and have a good time!'

So Brer Fox dragged the heavy can to and fro a good many times, whilst Brer Rabbit sat on the warm sunny wall and smoked his pipe and talked.

Now it wasn't long before Brer Bear and Brer Wolf came along and looked over the wall too.

'Heyo, Brer Rabbit,' said Brer Bear. 'We've just met Brer Terrapin, and he'd been a-boasting and a-bragging that you've let him fill up your pond because he's such an old friend of yours. And he said he was mighty certain you wouldn't give anyone else that treat – and here we see Brer Fox playing with the water too!'

'Oh, Brer Bear,' said Brer Rabbit politely, 'that's too bad of Brer Terrapin to go around saying I won't give any of my friends but him a chance to play with my pond. Brer Fox, he came along and said just the same thing – and I'm giving him a treat too! If you want to join in, you just say the word. I'm not the man to stop anyone having a good time!'

Well, by this time Brer Fox was nearly worn out with carrying the heavy can. So he spoke up at once.

'And I'm not the man to be selfish either. I'll let Brer Bear and Brer Wolf have a turn now. That's only fair!'

So Brer Wolf and Brer Bear came in at the gate and set to work to fill the can and empty the water into the pond. My, but it was nearly full now! It only needed about four more cans and it would overflow.

Cousin Wildcat looked over the wall and grinned. Brer Rabbit hopped off to the garden-seat, for he didn't trust Cousin Wildcat's claws.

'Heyo, Brer Rabbit,' said Cousin Wildcat. 'I just heard from Brer Terrapin that you've got Brer Fox and Brer Wolf and Brer Bear doing all your hard work for you. Ah, you're a smart one, Brer Rabbit, no doubt about that! But you don't catch me coming along and carrying your heavy cans for you all morning long. No – my brains are as good as yours *any* day, Brer Rabbit!'

Brer Fox, Brer Wolf, and Brer Bear stood and stared in surprise. Then they turned their eyes on Brer Rabbit, who began to feel mighty uncomfortable. But he put a bold face on it and spoke up well.

'Brer Fox! Brer Wolf! Brer Bear! Are you going to stand there, and let Cousin Wildcat make out I've tricked you, when all you've been doing is to have a treat? You go for him right now, and make him say he's sorry!'

So Brer Fox, Brer Wolf, and Brer Bear jumped over the wall and chased Cousin Wildcat right into the middle of the wood. He fled up a tree and laughed at them. 'Go and ask Brer Terrapin!' he cried. 'Maybe you'll believe *him*!'

But when the three of them hunted for Brer Terrapin, he was nowhere to be found! He was having a fine swim in Brer Rabbit's nice full pond – and every now and again he would come up to the top and wink his eye at Brer Rabbit. Then down he'd go to the bottom – ker-blinkety-blunk!

Brer Rabbit catches mice

Now once it happened that Brer Fox stored away some fine carrots and juicy turnips in his little old shed. He was mighty pleased with them, for he had grown them himself, and meant to have them in his soup that winter.

And of course old Brer Rabbit smelt them out, and made up his mind to share those carrots and turnips – though he didn't mean to ask Brer Fox's permission!

So, each night, he crept to the door of the shed and opened it quietly. In he went, and nibbled a carrot here, and a turnip there.

Well, Brer Fox was angry to find his stores nibbled like that. He stared round his shed each morning and wondered who the thief was. He saw Brer Rabbit passing by in the distance and he called to him.

'Heyo, Brer Rabbit! Do you know anything about nibbled carrots?'

'Nibbled carrots!' said wicked Brer Rabbit, pretending to be surprised. 'You don't mean to say you've got carrots in that shed that have been nibbled, Brer Fox?'

'That's just what I do mean to say,' said Brer Fox, looking at Brer Rabbit in a very straight way.

'It must be that you've got mice there,' said Brer Rabbit. 'I'd put a few mouse-traps down, Brer Fox, that's what I'd do!'

And with that old Brer Rabbit went off whistling, telling himself he must remember to look out for a mouse-trap when he went a-nibbling that night!

But Brer Fox didn't put any traps down. No, he kept awake himself, and when he heard the door of his shed creaking he jumped out of his chair and crept out into the garden. He went to his shed, and flashed his lantern inside.

Brer Rabbit had heard him coming – but he couldn't get out of the door in time. So what did he do but turn his back to the wall of the shed, and stick his bobtail out through a hole in the wood. And there he was a-sitting when Brer Fox popped his head in at the door!

'Oho, Brer Rabbit! So I've just caught you, have I!' said Brer Fox.

'What do you mean, caught me?' asked Brer Rabbit, in a most astonished voice. 'Here I've come to spend the whole night in your shed, to catch the mice that nibble your carrots – and you say you've caught me! That's not a nice way to repay a good deed, Brer Fox, and I'm really surprised at you.'

Brer Fox looked astonished. 'How are you catching mice for me?' he said.

'Why,' said Brer Rabbit, 'can't you see what I'm doing? I'm sitting here patiently with my tail out of a mouse-hole – and I'm waiting for a mouse to come along and nibble it – and then I'll pull in my tail like a shot and drag the mouse in at the hole for you!'

'I've never heard of that way of catching mice before,' said Brer Fox, looking even more astonished. 'Have you caught any yet?'

'Sh!' said Brer Rabbit. 'I think I can feel one a-nibbling!'

Brer Fox shushed. But after a time Brer Rabbit sighed and shook his head.

'No,' he said. 'That one ran away. It's a pity

my tail is so short, Brer Fox. Now, if I had a fine long one like yours, I'd catch twenty mice a night!'

'Would you really?' said Brer Fox, most interested. 'Well, what about me poking my tail out through a hole and seeing if I can catch some?'

'Oh, I wouldn't bother to do that,' said Brer Rabbit. 'You wouldn't have the patience to sit still long enough for a mouse to come.'

'Indeed I would,' said Brer Fox. 'I'm as patient as you are, any day.'

Well, in the end Brer Fox found a good big mouse-hole and stuck his tail out of it so that it twitched on the ground outside the shed. And there he sat, whilst Brer Rabbit sat near him, his bobtail out too.

'Ha! I can feel one a-nibbling!' said Brer Rabbit suddenly. 'Catch hold of my tail tightly, Mouse! Catch hold of it, I say!'

Brer Rabbit suddenly jerked his tail in and turned round to look at it as if he expected to see a mouse hanging on to the hairs. But there was nothing there, of course.

'Dear, dear!' said Brer Rabbit, sounding most

disappointed. 'What a pity! I made sure there was one that time. Keep still, Brer Fox, and see if he comes to your tail. And if you feel him a-nibbling, just call out, "Catch hold of my tail, there, catch hold of my tail!" '

Now, just about daybreak, as Brer Rabbit very well knew, Brer Bear came along that way. And that was what Brer Rabbit was planning for. He listened and he listened for Brer Bear's footsteps, and pretty soon he heard them – clump-clump-clump.

He began to talk so that Brer Fox wouldn't hear the footsteps. 'I can feel a mouse a-nibbling and a-gnawing!' he said. 'Catch hold of my tail, there, catch hold of my tail! You shout too, Brer Fox, in case there's one at your tail too.'

So Brer Fox shouted out, 'Catch hold of my tail, there, catch hold of my tail!'

And just at that moment Brer Bear passed the shed, and saw Brer Fox's tail hanging out of the hole, and he heard him shouting, 'Catch hold of my tail, there!'

'Funny thing!' said Brer Bear, sniffing at Brer Fox's tail, and touching it with his paw.

'It looks like Brer Fox's tail. But what is it doing here? And why should I catch hold of it?'

When Brer Fox felt Brer Bear sniffing at his tail, he got very excited, because he really thought it was a mouse at last.

'Catch hold of my tail, there!' he shouted. 'Catch hold of my tail!'

Brer Bear caught hold of his tail and held it

tight. Brer Fox suddenly looked most astonished. This couldn't be a mouse!

'Something's got my tail!' he said to Brer Rabbit in a scared voice. Brer Rabbit ran to the door when he heard that welcome news, for he knew that Brer Fox couldn't get away to go after him then. He shot out of the door.

'I'll go and see what it is that's got your tail!' he shouted – and he took a look at Brer Bear and winked.

'Hold on for a bit, Brer Bear!' he said. 'Hold on for a bit!' And with that he scampered away through the wood, lippitty-clippitty, and he didn't stop to laugh till he was safe at home with his door locked!

As for Brer Fox, there he had to stay in the shed till Brer Bear let go his tail. And what a quarrel there was then, to be sure, with Brer Fox calling Brer Bear names, and Brer Bear shouting at Brer Fox. They don't really know to this day that old Brer Rabbit played a mighty clever trick on them!

Brer Rabbit and the pears

One day, when Brer Rabbit trotted through the wood, he happened to see a little pear tree that was hung with large pears. He stopped and had a look at it.

'Those pears will be ripe next week,' he said to himself. 'And I'll be the one to pick them! My, won't they be juicy and sweet!'

So, the next week, he trotted by that way again and, sure enough, the pears were as ripe as could be. But somebody was up the tree picking them!

It was Brer Bear. Brer Bear liked a nice juicy apple or pear, and he had had his eye on that tree for a long time. And there he was, up in the tree, picking away as fast as he could, putting the ripe yellow pears into his basket, and now and then popping one whole into his big mouth.

Now Brer Rabbit wasn't in Brer Bear's good books at all just then, for he had taken some honey from a bee-tree that Brer Bear had specially wanted for himself. So it was quite a shock to Brer Rabbit to see Brer Bear there. He guessed Brer Bear wouldn't give him any of those pears just now.

Brer Rabbit looked at the little pear tree. He didn't like to climb up it in case Brer Bear pushed him down. No, that wouldn't do at all. But how in the world was he going to get any pears for himself?

Brer Rabbit sat and thought. Brer Bear hadn't seen him yet. Brer Rabbit crept off and went to Brer Terrapin's house under the water. He called down to him.

'Heyo, Brer Terrapin! Are you in this morning?'

'Oh yes, I'm in all right,' said Brer Terrapin, and he swam up to the top of the water. 'How are you feeling, Brer Rabbit?'

'Mighty hungry, Brer Terrapin,' said Brer Rabbit. 'Mighty hungry. And I've got a plan to get some fine juicy pears, if you'll come along and help me.'

Well, Brer Terrapin liked pears too, so he clambered out of the water, shook his feet, and they set off together. Brer Rabbit told Brer Terrapin his plan, and Brer Terrapin laughed till he nearly cracked his shell.

By and by they came up to the pear tree. Brer Bear was still up there, picking the pears. Brer Rabbit and Brer Terrapin sat down under the tree for all the world as if they didn't know anyone was there at all.

'Well, Brer Terrapin,' said Brer Rabbit in a loud voice, 'how's yourself?'

'Not too good, Brer Rabbit, not too good,' said Brer Terrapin. 'You know, ever since that tiresome Brer Bear tried to pull my tail out, I've had the trimble-trembles.'

'Oh, he's a bad fellow, Brer Bear is,' said Brer Rabbit. 'I'm no friend of his and he's no friend of mine.'

Now Brer Bear, sitting up in the tree, was most astonished and annoyed to hear all this. He sat there quietly, listening with both his ears.

'He's mean and he's selfish,' said Brer Terrapin loudly. 'That's what he is. And I wish he could hear me say so.'

Brer Rabbit stopped himself giggling. 'He's greedy too,' he said. 'Do you know, if he finds a

bee-tree, he never even offers me a sip of the honey there?'

Now this was a real story, for Brer Bear had often given Brer Rabbit a share of his honey. Brer Bear, he sat up in the tree boiling with rage, longing to get at Brer Rabbit and give him a good slap.

'He's a slow chap,' said Brer Terrapin. 'You call me slow, Brer Rabbit – but if I ran a race with Brer Bear I'd be at the winning-post before he was half-way there!'

'And he hasn't as many brains as a caterpillar,' said Brer Rabbit, enjoying himself. 'My, Brer Terrapin, what would Brer Bear say if he heard us talking like this about him?'

'What would he *do*?' giggled Brer Terrapin.

'I guess he'd throw something at us,' said Brer Rabbit. 'Yes, I guess that's what he'd do. Throw something at us, hard, and hit us! Ho ho! It's a good thing he isn't here, and hasn't got anything to throw!'

Well, this was too much altogether for Brer Bear. He gave a fierce growl, picked a large pear and threw it down the tree.

'I *am* here!' he grunted loudly. 'And I *have*

got something to throw! Take that – and that!'

Brer Rabbit and Brer Terrapin jumped up as if they were too astonished for anything. Brer Rabbit saw the pear coming and neatly caught it. The other one smashed on Brer Terrapin's shell. Brer Terrapin put out his head and began to lick it off with great delight.

'Goodness! It's Brer Bear up the tree!' said Brer Rabbit, pretending to be most upset and surprised. 'He's heard all we said! Brer Bear, Brer Bear, now just stop throwing things at us. You'll hurt us!'

'That's just what I mean to do, you nasty tale-telling creatures!' roared Brer Bear, feeling angrier and angrier. He took a pear from his basket and threw it straight at Brer Rabbit. 'Take that! Huh, I'll teach you to sit under a tree and talk like that about me! I'm throwing *this* pear for your storytelling – and *this* for your meanness – and *this* for your unkindness!'

Thud, plop, plop! Down came the pears! Some of them Brer Rabbit caught, others smashed on the ground and Brer Terrapin gobbled them up. One rolled away and Brer Rabbit picked it up.

'Stop, Brer Bear, stop! You'll hurt us!' cried Brer Rabbit, knowing quite well that Brer Bear would go on all the more if he were begged to stop. And so Brer Bear did. He was in such a rage that he threw down every pear in his basket, and picked every pear off the tree. Down they came, plop, plop, plop, and Brer Rabbit picked them up with glee.

At last there were no more pears left to throw. Brer Rabbit looked up and winked at Brer Bear.

'Well, you won't be wanting your basket now, will you?' he said. 'So what about throwing that down too, Brer Bear? It would be mighty useful for me to carry these pears home!'

And then Brer Bear knew that it was all a trick to get his pears, and he growled in rage. He began to climb down the tree, grunting and growling, and Brer Rabbit knew it was about time to go.

'Come on, Brer Terrapin,' he said. 'We've been here long enough. We'll go home.'

So off they went, the two of them – Brer Rabbit with his pockets crammed full of ripe pears, and Brer Terrapin with his shell dripping with pear juice. My, how they giggled when they thought of Brer Bear throwing down his pears! Wicked Brer Rabbit – whatever will he do next?

Brer Bear gets a shock

One time Brer Bear went to look at his honey store and he found that half his honey-jars were empty. Well, he ranted and he roared, he howled and he stamped, and he vowed he'd find the thief if it took him a month of Sundays.

He went stamping out of his house, and who should he meet but old Brer Wolf, come to see if Brer Bear was away from home – for Brer Wolf liked a lick of honey himself, and he was the thief all right!

'Someone's been at my honey, Brer Wolf – someone's been at my honey!' roared Brer Bear. 'Who do you think it can be? I'm just going to squeeze the life out of him!'

Brer Wolf looked alarmed. He didn't want to be squeezed in Brer Bear's big arms! 'Well,' he said, 'I saw that rascal of a Brer Rabbit the other day with honey on his whiskers. Ah yes, Brer Bear, sure enough you'll find it's Brer Rabbit who's the thief!'

'I thought as much!' yelled Brer Bear in a rage. 'He's always where he shouldn't be. But he's played his tricks once too often!'

He rushed off to find Brer Rabbit, and as he went through the wood, what did he see but old Brer Rabbit sitting on a tree-stump combing his fine whiskers.

'Are you combing the honey out of your whiskers?' shouted Brer Bear, and he rushed at Brer Rabbit.

'Now, now, Brer Bear!' cried Brer Rabbit, in

alarm, as Brer Bear knocked him over. 'What's the matter? Can't I comb my whiskers?'

'Not if they've got my honey on them!' roared Brer Bear angrily. 'I'm going to squeeze you, Brer Rabbit – yes, I'm going to squeeze you, and make you say where you've put all my honey!'

Brer Wolf crept up and saw the fight. He rubbed his paws in glee, for he guessed that old Brer Rabbit wouldn't come bobbing up *this* time! Brer Bear got hold of Brer Rabbit and began to hug him so that he couldn't breathe.

'Stop it, Brer Bear, stop it!' panted poor Brer Rabbit. 'I tell you, I don't know anything about your honey.'

'Now you just tell me where you've put my honey and I'll let you go,' said Brer Bear. 'Go on – tell me. If you don't, I'll squeeze you to bits!'

Well, Brer Rabbit could see that Brer Bear meant what he said all right, and he began to think how he could stop him.

'Brer Bear, Brer Bear, how can I tell you where your honey is if you squeeze all my breath out of me!' panted Brer Rabbit.

Brer Bear stopped squeezing quite so hard. 'Will you tell me, Brer Rabbit?' he said.

'Brer Bear, I'm not certain where your honey is, but I think maybe you'll get a nice surprise if you look into that hollow tree that's growing by the pond in the wood,' said Brer Rabbit, trying to get his breath again.

'Are you sure I shall get a surprise if I look there?' asked Brer Bear squeezing Brer Rabbit tightly again.

'Brer Bear, stop hugging me!' begged Brer Rabbit in alarm. 'You're squeezing my chest right through my back! I tell you, you will surely get a fine surprise if you look inside that tree!'

Brer Bear let Brer Rabbit go. He ambled off to the tree, and Brer Wolf and Brer Rabbit followed him, though poor Brer Rabbit could hardly walk.

Well, Brer Bear, he got to the hollow tree all right. He climbed up to where the hole was, and put in his paw. But it was a very deep hole and he could feel nothing.

'Get down into the hole, Brer Bear, get down into the hole!' squealed Brer Rabbit. So Brer

Bear jumped right down into the hole, and pawed about for the honey.

But in that hole lived Cousin Wildcat, his wife and his family – and when old Brer Bear jumped right down up top of the lot of them, there was a great disturbance!

My goodness! All those wildcats shot out their twenty claws, and clawed at Brer Bear. Cousin Wildcat and his wife buried their sharp teeth into his paws, and before Brer Bear knew what was happening he was in the middle of a fierce fight!

'Oooph! Grumph! Ow-wow-wow!' growled Brer Bear.

'Yee-ow-yee-ow, yee-ow!' yelled all the wild-cats together.

Brer Bear shot out of that hollow tree a whole lot quicker than he went in! My, how quickly he came out! Brer Rabbit had never seen a bear move so quickly!

'You said I'd find my honey there!' roared Brer Bear to Brer Rabbit.

'I didn't!' yelled back cheeky Brer Rabbit. 'I just said you'd get a fine surprise if you looked in that hollow tree. But if you want to find the

thief, Brer Bear, just come and look at Brer Wolf here! He's got honey on his nose – and I guess he's been after yours!'

And with that Brer Rabbit turned and ran, and old Brer Wolf, he got such a slap on the nose from angry Brer Bear that he yowled like a hundred wildcats at once!

As for Brer Bear, he wouldn't go near a hollow tree for months, not even when he saw bees coming out of it and knew there was honey there. No – he was much too afraid of getting another fine surprise!

Brer Rabbit and the butter

It happened once that the creatures made a lot of very fine butter, and they agreed to put it into a cool shed, and share it between them.

But Brer Rabbit wasn't to have any at all, because he was such a rascal. Brer Fox winked all round and said, 'That will teach old Brer Rabbit to stop tricking us! When he doesn't get his butter, he'll be sorry!'

Now Brer Rabbit was as angry as a dozen wildcats when he heard that he wasn't to share in the butter. He sat in his house and he scratched first one ear and then the other, trying to think of some way he could get that butter.

Well, he guessed if he went along that way at night he'd get that butter all right! So each night Brer Rabbit slid between the trees and came to the shed where the butter was kept. He opened the door, went to the butter-pail and scooped out a nice pat of butter. Then off he went as quietly as he had come.

Now when the creatures found their butter going every night, they knew there was a thief somewhere. And they guessed it was their old friend, Brer Rabbit!

'We'll set a trap for him!' said Brer Fox, grinning. 'That's what we'll do. We'll spread the shed-floor with black soot, and old Brer Rabbit won't see it in the dark! It will get on to his shoes, and in the morning we'll see a sooty track leading back to his house – then we'll all know who the thief is!'

Well, everyone thought that was a fine idea, and Brer Wolf, he swept his chimney, put the soot into a sack and took it along to the butter-shed. He spread the floor with the soot and went away.

Now that night along came Brer Rabbit as usual for his pat of butter. It was dark and he couldn't see the soot – but he could smell it all right! Oh yes, Brer Rabbit knew the smell of fresh soot, and he stood there in the shed and sniffed hard.

'Soot on the floor!' said Brer Rabbit, and he

grinned to himself. 'Put there to catch me! Ha, they think they'll see my sooty footsteps leading to my house – and they'll come and say I steal the butter. No, no, Brer Fox, you can't trick me so easily as that!'

Brer Rabbit took his pat of butter and skipped out on his sooty feet. He walked as heavily as he could to a tree. Then he took off his sooty shoes and pressed them hard against the tree-trunk so that it looked for all the world as if someone had been walking up there!

Then Brer Rabbit skipped home in his bare feet, carrying the shoes, as happy as a jay-bird!

The next morning the creatures were excited to see the sooty footmarks. They all followed them till they came to the tree, and they were *most* astonished to see the footprints going up the trunk!

'Queer!' said Brer Fox, looking hard at them.

'The thief must live up in this tree,' said Brer Wolf, peering up. 'But only Cousin Wildcat lives in trees.'

'Well, one of us must go up and see who lives here,' said Brer Bear. 'Brer Turkey-Buzzard, you fly up and see what you can find.'

So Brer Turkey-Buzzard flew up, but though he spent hours looking into every hole and along every branch, he simply could *not* find the thief!

Well, the next night Brer Rabbit skipped along for his butter again, and walked hard on the soot. When he left the shed he walked along to the bank of the river. Then he took off his shoes and ran along home in his bare feet once more.

The next day all the animals found the sooty footprints once again, and followed them with glee. This time they would surely find the thief!

'The footmarks stop just here!' said Brer Fox in astonishment, and he pointed to the bank of the river. 'Maybe Brer Terrapin, or his Uncle Mud-Turtle, is the thief!'

'Indeed we're not!' said Brer Terrapin, who had come along with the others. 'Last night we were at a party at Mr Benjamin Ram's, as he'll tell you. We didn't go near the butter-shed!'

'Well, it's a strange thing,' said Brer Wolf, puzzled. 'First those footsteps lead us to a tree – and now they lead us to a river!'

The next night Brer Rabbit fetched his butter and danced off in his sooty shoes. He skipped along till he came to the middle of a field, then he took off his shoes and ran home.

And when the creatures found the footmarks stopping in the middle of the field, they looked at one another in amazement.

'Well, the thief must have wings!' said Brer Fox. 'He couldn't just disappear like that! I wonder if it's Brer Turkey-Buzzard.'

'No, it isn't,' said Brer Turkey-Buzzard indignantly. 'I was away at my uncle's all last night, as he will tell you.'

Now just then along came old Brer Rabbit, and he saw all the animals looking puzzled and talking to one another. So he skipped up and said how-do to them.

'What's puzzling you?' he asked. 'You tell me, and I'll help you!'

So they told him about the missing butter, and how they couldn't make out who the thief was because one time he walked up a tree, and another time he went into the river, and the third time he just disappeared in the middle of a field!

'You let *me* keep your butter for you in *my* shed and it'll be all right!' said Brer Rabbit. 'I guess no thief will dare to come around tricking *me*! You let *me* take care of the butter!'

'Well, we'll pay you a pat of butter each day if you'll keep the thief away,' said Brer Fox. 'But if you don't, you won't get any butter, Brer Rabbit!'

'You trust me to keep the thief away!' grinned old Brer Rabbit. 'I won't need any soot to catch him either! The thief's afraid of me! I'm fierce, I am, and no one will take your butter!'

So the butter was moved to Brer Rabbit's shed, and the creatures gave him a large piece of it every day for keeping it safe. No thief came near it, of course, so the creatures were very pleased.

'Oh, Brer Rabbit's a mighty fierce fellow!' they said to each other. 'No thief dares to get our butter now!'

And they wondered why old Brer Rabbit grinned when he heard them. He's a rascal, isn't he?

Brer Fox's new house

It happened once that old Brer Fox got himself a fine new house. My, wasn't he proud of it too! He called it Bushy Villa, after his tail, and he got Mrs Bear to make him some blue curtains.

Now Brer Rabbit had wanted the house for himself, and he was in a great rage when he found that Brer Fox had walked in and taken it.

He set off to the house and knocked at the door, blim-blam!

'Who's there?' called Brer Fox.

'Brer Rabbit!' said Brer Rabbit.

'Come right in, Brer Rabbit!' sang out Brer Fox. But Brer Rabbit knew better than that. He just stood out there on the doorstep and shouted.

'Brer Fox! I'd like this house myself. I've come to offer you a good price for it.'

'Then you can think again, Brer Rabbit,' said Brer Fox, pleased to find that he had got something that Brer Rabbit wanted. 'I'm in this house and here I stay! Good morning to you!'

Brer Rabbit was in a fine rage. He set off home, thinking with all his brains – and he had a good many. As he went along, head down and ears up, who should he meet but Brer Terrapin, the same old one-and-sixpence!

'How-do, Brer Rabbit,' yelled out Brer Terrapin. 'Look where you're going!'

'How-do, Brer Terrapin!' said Brer Rabbit, stopping and grinning at his old friend. 'Why, Brer Terrapin, you are just the person I want to see. I've got a plan.'

Brer Terrapin walked along by Brer Rabbit, listening to his plan of getting Brer Fox out of the house.

'You see, Brer Terrapin, if I can frighten him away, he'll sell it to me,' said Brer Rabbit. 'Now what about me sitting up on the roof and hanging things down the chimney when Brer Fox is sitting there reading his paper? Don't you think that would give him a shock?'

'I should just think it would!' said Brer Terrapin. 'And what about me sitting there with him that evening and pretending I can't see anything coming down the chimney? That would be funnier still.'

So it was arranged that Brer Terrapin should drop in at Brer Fox's house the next evening, and that Brer Rabbit should sit up on the roof with a fishing-line and drop things down on the end of the string.

'I'll tie my old tin teapot on first,' giggled Brer Rabbit. 'Then I'll tie an old boot. And then I'll tie Brer Fox's own hat. I'll slip into the hall and get it, once you are sitting talking to him, Brer Terrapin. That will give him a shock all right!'

Well, the next evening Brer Terrapin ambled along to Brer Fox's, and knocked at the door, blim, blam! Brer Fox was pleased to see him and asked him in.

'I've got a good fire, Brer Terrapin,' he said. 'Come along in and warm your toes.'

As soon as they were safely in the parlour, Brer Rabbit crept into the hall and took Brer Fox's best hat. Then, with his old tin teapot under his arm, and a dirty old boot and his fishing-line in his pocket, he climbed quietly up to the roof. He sat beside the chimney and cocked his ear up to hear what Brer Terrapin was saying to Brer Fox.

'You know, Brer Fox,' Brer Terrapin was saying, 'this house feels kind of funny to me. I guess I wouldn't like to live in it myself!'

'Pooh!' said Brer Fox; 'you don't know what you are talking about, Brer Terrapin. This house is just an ordinary, comfortable place, with nothing queer about it at all.'

'There'll be something queer mighty soon!' said Brer Rabbit to himself, and he tied the tin teapot on to the end of his line. He dropped the line carefully down the chimney, and the teapot rattled against the bricks all the way down, clitter-clatter, clitter-clatter!

Brer Fox heard the noise and looked surprised. Brer Terrapin sucked at his old pipe and pretended to hear nothing at all. Down the chimney came the tin teapot and swung over the flames, just near Brer Fox's nose.

Brer Fox stared as if he couldn't believe his eyes. A teapot! Down the chimney! Hanging there as if by magic! Now what could be the meaning of that?

He spoke to Brer Terrapin in a low voice.

'Brer Terrapin! What do you suppose that tin teapot is doing in my chimney?'

Brer Terrapin turned and stared at Brer Fox as if he were greatly surprised. 'Tin teapot!' he said. 'What are you talking about, Brer Fox? Tin teapot, indeed! You'll be telling me it's dancing a jig next!'

Brer Rabbit, up on the roof, grinned when he heard that. He at once jerked his line and the teapot jumped up and down for all the world as if it were dancing a jig. Brer Fox clutched his whiskers and groaned.

'It *is* dancing a jig!' he said. 'Brer Terrapin, do just look! Surely you can see a tin teapot dancing about in the chimney?'

Brer Terrapin turned towards the chimney and shut his eyes. 'No,' he said truthfully, 'I can't see any teapot there, Brer Fox. Are you playing a joke on me?'

The teapot disappeared, and Brer Fox heaved a sigh. 'Well, it's gone now,' he said. 'What a peculiar thing! A teapot in my chimney, and you don't see it, Brer Terrapin!'

'Don't you tell that kind of story to an old chap like me,' said Brer Terrapin, settling himself more comfortably in his chair. 'It's no good you expecting me to believe tales of teapots, Brer Fox, nor of anything else either!'

Slither-slither-slosh! Down the chimney came the old boot, tied tightly to the end of the string! Brer Fox leapt up from his chair in fright and stared at it.

'There's a boot now!' he cried. 'Can't you see it, Brer Terrapin?'

'No, that I can't,' said Brer Terrapin, looking at the chimney with his eyes shut again. 'I can't see a thing. Do sit down, Brer Fox, and don't keep jumping and shouting. You make me quite uncomfortable.'

'Well, I'm not used to teapots and boots jiggling in my chimney-place,' said Brer Fox fiercely. 'You said there was something funny about this house, Brer Terrapin, and so there is. I don't like it.'

'Sit down, Brer Fox, sit down,' begged Brer Terrapin, sucking at his pipe. 'How can a man enjoy his pipe when you keep shouting about teapots and boots I can't see? Don't be silly.'

The boot disappeared. Brer Fox stared at the chimney-place for a while and then sat down on

the edge of his seat, watching the chimney. No sooner had he sat down than the boot slithered down again, and poor Brer Fox shot out of his seat, fell over Brer Terrapin, and sat down heavily on the floor.

Brer Terrapin wanted to laugh but he dared not. 'Goodness gracious, Brer Fox, what are you doing now?' he said. 'Something else come down the chimney? Well, well, well, I don't know what you wanted to buy this house for! I heard that Brer Rabbit wanted it, and I'm sure I don't know why you didn't let him have it.'

'I don't know why either,' groaned Brer Fox. 'I'd sell it to him now, I know that!'

Brer Rabbit grinned in delight. He tied the fine new hat on to the end of his line, and let that down the chimney too. Swish-swish-swish it came, sweeping all the soot on to the brim as it went, so that Brer Fox's fine hat looked very sorry for itself when at last it appeared in the fireplace.

Brer Fox stared in horror. 'Look, Brer Terrapin, look!' he said. 'There's my new hat! Oh, my, oh my, it's my new hat! I can't bear it! I can't bear it!'

Brer Rabbit leant right over the chimney and nearly burst himself with laughing. But he didn't know what was going to happen next! Brer Fox was so wild at seeing his beautiful new hat dancing in the chimney covered with soot that he suddenly made a dart at it and caught hold of it! He pulled hard – and Brer Rabbit overbalanced and fell right into the chimney himself! Down he went, slither-swish, and landed in the hearth. He gave a great yell when he sat on the flames, and shot off like a bullet out of a gun!

Even Brer Terrapin got a shock that time, and he ran out of the house faster than any terrapin ran before. Brer Fox was scared too, for he wondered what was coming down the chimney *this* time! But when he saw it was Brer Rabbit, he was after him like lightning.

And Brer Rabbit lost a few hairs out of his tail that night, he was so nearly caught. He didn't get Brer Fox's house after all, and how he shook his fist when Brer Fox met him and called after him, 'Hie! Sweep! Would you like to come and do my chimneys for me?'

Aha, Brer Rabbit, you didn't win *that* time!